William Renton

Songs of William Renton

William Renton

Songs of William Renton

ISBN/EAN: 9783337007348

Printed in Europe, USA, Canada, Australia, Japan

Cover: Foto ©Thomas Meinert / pixelio.de

More available books at **www.hansebooks.com**

SONGS

OF

WILLIAM RENTON

London
T. FISHER UNWIN
PATERNOSTER SQUARE
MDCCCXCIII

CONTENTS.

	PAGE
A SONG OF MIDSUMMER	1
A SONG OF THE JESSAMINE	3
A SONG OF THE GOLDEN RIVER	5
A SONG OF THE BRIDE-CHAMBER	8
A SONG OF A LOVER	10
A SONG OF DUSK	11
A SONG OF VIGIL	13
A SONG OF THE DEPTHS	16
A SONG OF THE NIGHT	17
A SONG OF SAD HEART	20
A SONG OF THE BALCONY	27
SONGS OF THE BELOVED	29
A SONG BETWEEN TWO KISSES	33
A SONG OF ROSY LIPS	36
A SONG OF KISSES	37
A SONG OF RESERVE	42
A SONG OF ENTREATY	44
A SONG OF LOVE	45
A SONG OF FAREWELL	47
A SONG OF THE SEA	52
A SONG OF SYMPATHY	57
A SONG OF THREE	61
A SONG OF THE MILL	62
A SONG OF FOUR	64

	PAGE
A SONG OF THE HERMITAGE . . .	65
CHANSON DE LA TROP BIEN AIMÉE . .	67
A SONG OF A DAY	68
A SONG FROM AFAR	70
A SONG OF THE YOUNG MOON . . .	71
A SONG OF THE DREAMLESS LAND . .	74
A SONG OF A CHRISTMAS ROSE . . .	75
A SONG OF THE LAKE	78
A SONG OF THE SANDS	79
CHANSON SANS PAROLES . . .	81
A SONG OF A VOICE	82
A SONG TO THE SINGER . . .	83
A SONG OF COURAGE	84
A SONG OF RHYMES	86
SONGS OF SYMBOLS	88

SONNETS.

A SONG OF DIFFERENTIALS . . .	89
A SONG OF INTEGRALS	90
A SONG OF BEAUTY . . .	91
A SONG OF THE ANTIQUE . . .	92
A SONG OF POESY	93
A SONG OF THE REVERSE . . .	94
A SONG OF A SONG	95
A SONG OF DISCOVERY . . .	96
A SONG OF PASSION	97
A SONG OF LIGHT-LOVE . . .	98
A SONG OF DESIRE	99
A SONG OF THE EYES	100

	PAGE
A SONG OF PARTS OF SPEECH	101
A SONG OF THE OPERA	102
A SONG OF HAND IN HAND	103
A SONG OF CHANGE	104
A SONG OF SELF-POSSESSION	105
A SONG OF HEED	106
A SONG OF NAMES	107
A SONG OF THE FOURTH COMMANDMENT	108
A SONG OF DEFIANCE	109
CHANSON DE DÉFI	110
A SONG OF SOLICITUDE	111
A SONG OF CROSS-PURPOSE	112
A SONG OF PARTING	113
A SONG OF BEQUEST	114
A SONG OF COMPARISON	115
A SONG OF REVERSION	116
A SONG OF THE SOUTH-WEST WIND	117
A SONG OF THE VINTAGE	118
A SONG OF THE WARDROBE	119
A SONG OF THE BEDCHAMBER	120
A SONG TO BEDWARD	121
A SONG OF SOLITUDE	122
SONGS OF THE EARLY DEAD	123
A SONG OF INTERSPACE	128

ROUNDELS AND BALLADS.

A SONG OF SONGS	129
SONGS OF SONG	130
A SONG OF A SMILE	134

	PAGE
SONGS OF A PORTRAIT	135
A SONG OF DEVOTION	137
A SONG OF LENT	138
SONGS OF ENVOI	139
SONGS OF ABSENCE	141
A SONG OF WELCOME	143
A SONG OF RETURN	144
CHANSON DU BAISER PERDU	145
SONGS OF THE NEST	146
A SONG OF SWEET LIPS	148
SONGS OF THE ROSE	149
A SONG OF BEATING HEART	153
SONGS OF THE STARLIGHT	154
A SONG OF PARDON	156
A SONG AT BEST	157
A SONG OF DREAMLAND	158
A SONG OF UNREQUITAL	159
A SONG OF THE VANISHED	160
SONGS OF DESOLATION	161
A SONG OF TRUTH	166
SONGS OF THE POETS	167
A SONG FOR BREAKFAST	171
A SONG IN DUDGEON	172
A SONG OF SCORN	173
A SONG FOR MY DARLING	175
A SONG OF DAYDREAM	177
A SONG OF THE DANCE	179
A SONG OF THE VINEYARD	181
A SONG OF YES AND NO	183

A SONG OF MIDSUMMER.

IT is summer in the skies,
    Very noontide of Cathay;
If you fear it for your eyes,
    There are haycocks in the hay:
Come and watch the butterflies,
    Come away.

Ah what odours in the heat
    Float from field and porch and spray!
Stars of jasmine for your feet,
    White and scented as the May,
Fall around the garden seat:
    Come away.

Butterflies of white divine
    Fan the odours, faint as they,
From the sleeping jessamine;
    Be their darling for to-day,
Be their sweet, as thou art mine:
    Come away.

There shall be no marvel there,
   But a girl with eyes astray
In a bower of jasmine fair,
   And a boy beside her gay
Weaving jasmine in her hair:
   Come away.

We shall hear the river pour,
   Waking with its idle lay
All the windings of the shore;
   We shall think we hear it say
Nevermore and *Evermore:*
   Come away.

As upon a gateway steep
   Children swing themselves in play,
We will swing upon the deep
   Soothing sense of holiday;
We will sing ourselves to sleep:
   Come away.

A SONG OF THE JESSAMINE.

KISS and cling, kiss and cling
    Close to me, Darling, to-night ;
Clasp and cling, clasp and cling,
    Warm in the pale moonlight ;
Bound to me here with a golden ring,
Turn to the silent moon and sing
    Under the jessamine white :
*Bright as the jessamine, light as the
    jessamine blows.*

Rich and rife, rich and rife,
    Here by the red rose in flower,
Rare and rife, rare and rife
    Blossoms our jessamine bower ;
Jessamine hues with the rose at strife,
All for the love of the perfect wife,
    Mine at this perfect hour :
*Mine with the jessamine, mine and mine
    with the rose.*

Passing sweet, passing sweet
    Under the white moonshine,
Kisses sweet, kisses sweet
    Gives me my darling mine,
Fleet as the jessamine scents are fleet ;
I will fall down and kiss her feet,
    Her kisses are better than wine :
*Kisses no red rose, kisses no jessamine
    knows.*

A SONG OF THE GOLDEN RIVER.

TO the Golden River : The dream leads
 By silver brakes and saffron meads;
Nor sun, nor any moon, nor sense
Of shade, nor any need of shade;
Only a mystic influence,
That like a rolling music speeds
The wayfarer from glade to glade.

To the Golden River : No sign to tell
What pathway leads from dell to dell;
Each sees a glory all his own
In following, and of all the host
Each seems unto himself foremost,
For all are under golden spell,
Each deems himself to move alone.

To the Golden River: Do they know
To what a clime indeed they go,
Who wander under goodly skies
Within the golden afterglow,
The spirit risen in their eyes,
And on their moving lips the soul,
And on their brow the aureole?

To the Golden River: Some have told
A golden river runs of old,
A river of hope and golden dream,
And golden shadows in the stream,
And golden eddies in the gold,
And breaks on many a golden shoal;
The river runs from pole to pole.

To the Golden River: The land lies
Beyond the sunset, they surmise;
For when the afterglow is dead
They hope to find the journey done,
Nor ever more to see the sun,
Nor any flush of evening-red,
Nor any rainbow at sunrise.

To the Golden River: Hand in hand
With their own day-dreams, through the land
They wander on and on for ever
To glamour and the golden sand,
To voices in the golden weeds,
And, lettered on the golden reeds,
The legend of the Golden River.

A SONG OF THE BRIDE-CHAMBER.

THEY come from under orange bowers,
    Whose voices hush across the land;
  They stand together hand in hand:
It is the time of orange flowers.

The wind blows softly from a south
    Of orange gardens by the stream;
  He comes as from a perfumed dream,
An orange blossom in his mouth.

She finds him sweet, she speaks him fair,
    The all-expected wedding guest,
  Who showers the favours from his breast
In orange blossoms on her hair.

He shakes them down to brim the tide
    When kisses fall from mouth to mouth,
  Like orchard blossoms in the south
Upon the river far and wide.

And so they loosen from the land :
　The boat glides under festal showers,
　As heaven might fall in orange flowers :
And sail for ever hand in hand.

A SONG OF A LOVER.

TALL Fair and Sweet: what would you
   more than this?
He risks but loss that would have more
   than all,
And, niggard fool, doth find it his amiss
   Who finds her less than Fair and Sweet
   and Tall.

Fair Sweet and Tall: who that hath seen
   her pass
At morning like a garden through the air
But finds her very image in the glass
   A foil to her for Sweet and Tall and
   Fair?

Sweet Tall and Fair: he that did spite her
   nigh
For favour of some passing counterfeit
Now sees t'was *She*, and in despite would
   die
   To find her here so Tall and Fair and
   Sweet.

A SONG OF DUSK.

PALE sweet Face on the path by the
  wood in the twilight,
 Impalpable Face under the pale sweet
  skies,
Lit with the one star hung between low
  light and high light,
 Lit with the glamour of languid ineffable
  eyes.

Shadowy Form, half hid from the eyes
  that would scan it,
 Hid from the night in the light of its
  mystic grace,
Mounting with stately steps and slow, like
  the planet
 That loves and burns in the deeps of the
  twilit space.

Into the light from the dark, from the love
    and the lover,
  Hand thrust to my lips, eyes looking
    light upon mine,
Eyes dark in the light that closes around
    and above her,
  Light that is dark in the light of her
    eyes divine.

Into the dark from the light I go where I
    found her,
  My soul with the flame of her presence
    athirst and astir ;
And the night is a dream and a glory
    above and around her,
  And the paths of the wood, though she
    speaks not, are filled with the music
    of her.

A SONG OF VIGIL.

FROM the garden your orchard encloses,
    By the fountain across the lawn,
I have watched all night with the roses,
    And the breeze is awake with the fawn ;
In the dream where thy spirit reposes
    Is it dawn with thee, Sweet, is it dawn ?

You leaned last night from the casement,
    We kissed and we said adieu ;
The moon drew back in amazement,
    And I ask myself still, Is it true ?
And I watch and I walk by the basement
    And am dreaming and dreaming of you.

With fingers soft as a shed rose
    You pressed my fingers light,
And I kissed your lips of the red rose,
    I kissed your eyes of the white ;
Is your promise dead as the dead rose,
    Or will you come back to-night ?

O night and O frosts that harden
  And chill the importunate blood,
Shall I ask my Lady to pardon
  A trespass herself has made good?
The bird that is bid to the garden
  Should scarce take wing to the wood.

And the night like a dream in its might
    rose,
  And the stars were asleep saving three,
And the moon went down as the night
    rose,
  And the wind murmured faint from the
    sea;
The red rose slept with the white rose,
  And I thought, Would she wake with
    me?

Ah hope, thou swallow in Maytime,
  Thy wings are too eager for flight;
If we bring thee a whip in thy playtime
  Thou wilt scourge and scorn us outright;
And love is a child in the daytime
  If he grows to a giant at night.

So, Sweet, it is well my heart still is
   As a fruit in your garden that grows,
To pluck or to leave as your will is,
   As a flower to open or close,
Whether fasting all night with the lilies
   Or feasting at dawn with the rose.

Can the dove you have fed with caresses
   But return to be fed and caressed?
The falcon, inured to your jesses,
   How should he fly back to the nest?
O be sure who hath fingered your tresses
   Will long to lay hand on your breast.

Take counsel, Love, ere thou repliest,
   Lest the morning be pledge for the night;
It is well for hope at his nighest
   That his features are hidden from sight;
But say, what is love at the highest,
   If this be love at the height?

A SONG OF THE DEPTHS.

DEEP calls to deep within these eyes of
    thine,
  The solemn silence of two nights that
    keep
A day between them; and, as in a shrine
  Where tapers burn and mystic odours
    weep,
Mine eyes, their priests and worshippers,
    incline
  Their light before them, and deep calls
    to deep.

Still bend on me that dark and light
    divine,
  Till night shall call to night, and sleep
    to sleep;
And in thy dreams mixed with these
    dreams of mine
  Deep answers deep.

A SONG OF THE NIGHT.

SWEET ah sweet in her white-rose bower,
　Warm as the brood in the ringdove's nest,
　Hushed like the bee in the rose's breast
Hid for his hour;

Sweet in her arms in the moonless air
　To listen and dream of the long caress
　That never comes but to heal and bless,
Kissing her hair;

One hand laid on the tender wrist,
　As a yellow rose on a rose of white,
　Light as a kiss on the fingers light
Fain to be kissed;

One, caressing the curl that blows
   Vague as a tendril of the vine,
   Veiling the flame of her cheek from mine,
Roseleaf by rose.

One red rose in that white rose land
   Never a bee may come nigh to kiss,
   Never a lip touch, sweet as it is,
Never a hand.

One sweet thirst in the flower's deep heart
   Will never be stilled or stirred by me:
   Thy perfume, what availeth it thee,
Musk rose that art?

What of the night, Love? Ask of the night;
   What should it know of the hope that is born,
   The fear that is dead, what of anger, of scorn,
What of delight?

Kiss me, Child, ere the night grows cold ;
  Lest we weary here, playing a part,
  Feeding for ever upon the heart
Of a love grown old.

What is love's watchword? Answer, delight ;
  What should he know of the fear that is born,
  The hope that is dead, of the noon, of the morn,
What of the night?

Press me once more upon eyes and heart,
  The stars are dim and the night is old ;
  Thy kiss is warm, if thy lips are cold,
Take hands and part.

A SONG OF SAD HEART.

GOOD night, Sad Heart, good night.
   Strange welcome we have had,
   That makes the heart so sad
Which was so light.

The moon sets calm as fate:
   A young and tender moon
   Like thee, who went so soon
And came so late.

Sweet, what has come between?
   Why is our summer turned
   To frost, our sunset burned
From red to green?

Was it a stolen delight?
   Was it a whispered fear?
   Why are we wretched here,
We two, to-night?

Why this pale face of care?
  No snowdrop and no snow
  Hath anything to show
So pure, so fair.

Time has not such another,
  My lily in the green,
  That unto me hast been
Sister to brother.

I know it, I, thy friend:
  No sister is like thee,
  My Sister, nor will be
World without end.

O sad sweet Heart and sore,
  I read it in thine eyes,
  The one word born of sighs,
The Nevermore.

You do not need to speak:
  I see the night's eclipse
  In the cold eyes, the lips,
And the cold cheek.

Is that the foot I kissed
   That is so strange to-day?
   Is that the hand that lay
In mine, the wrist?

Is that the face so white
   That was so warm at dusk,
   The lips that were like musk
But yesternight?

How I did drink my fill
   At these full eyes and life!
   Thy very finger-tips
Are on me still.

How I did bathe my cheek
   In the warm bath of thine!
   Our kisses burned like wine;
We did not speak;

But each in each did rest,
   Tranced for that hour apart,
   Breast beating against heart,
Heart against breast.

You sat upon my knee,
  Do you remember now?
  Your hair against my brow;
From you to me

It was one interchange
  Of kisses: kisses mild
  And sweet, and kisses wild
And sweet and strange;

When lips for very bliss
  Yearned till the lips beneath
  Parted and left the teeth
Alone to kiss.

Ah I remember well
  The softness of your feet,
  How sweet your lips, how sweet
Your hair to smell.

And this, is this the end?
  Must Love's own hand unweave
  Love's silken web, and leave
Only the Friend?

O surely, Sweet, full soon
　　There will be end of night,
　　We shall find fairer light,
A fuller moon.

That it should come to this!
　　To have no heart to tell
　　Our love, who loved so well,
Scarce even to kiss.

And so I take your hand;
　　Time flies, our lips are shut,
　　We scarce can speak it, but
We understand.

This is no time for love.
　　One kiss! You must not stand
　　To speak. What a cold hand!
Where is your glove?

See, all my head is bare
　　Before you, as your calm
　　Clear voice rings like a psalm
In the chill air:

" Yes, we can always write,
　　And take hands now and then,
　　And kiss, but not again
As yesternight."

Yes, yes, my Child. Run, run!
　　I should—the night is late—
　　Have seen you to the gate,
But now not one

Of the old ways may be :
　　He that has done with heaven
　　Has done with earth, and even
With courtesy.

I that had been thy path
　　To walk on, died to be
　　Pressed by the foot of thee,
Must now in wrath

Turn from thee, like a hound
　　Bidden go home. Ah well,
　　How near to heaven is hell,
The world how round !

Here on this very spot
  We parted nine weeks since.
  Great Heaven! nine weeks *hence*
Is all forgot?

Here on this very walk—
  O fool why not let be
  Thy bliss, thy misery?
Why talk, why talk?

Truce to thy vanity!
  Shall Time travail in pain,
  Change kingdoms, yet remain
The same to thee?

Well, well, I shall not weep,
  For all my heart is chill
  As thine, dear Love; I will
Go home and sleep.

And so my Life, my Light,
  My Spirit and Soul that art,
  My own sweet sad Sweetheart,
Once more, good night.

A SONG OF THE BALCONY.

HERE by your balcony I stand,
    Once more, once more, my Sweet,
And close upon the plighted land
    Where moon and ivy greet ;
For here one night you kissed my hand,
    And here I kissed your feet.

The dawn, her starry chariots manned,
    With all her coursers fleet,
Drives down toward the silver strand
    Where earth and ocean meet,
To stay the pressure of your hand,
    The imprint of your feet.

Earth's million million tongues command,
    Her million eyes entreat
The rocket, soaring like a brand
    To shower in golden sleet,
To rise once more to kiss your hand,
    And, falling, kiss your feet.

Each organ by fair fingers spanned
  In every mystic beat
Gives out, what all yon glorious band
  Upon the pane repeat,
The music of your heavenly hand,
  The music of your feet.

The hourglass in her garb of sand
  Falling half incomplete
Recalls the scene, by moonlight scanned,
  When with a touch discreet
The robe from your unrobing hand
  Falls on your still robed feet.

O from what moonset of what land
  Where night and morning greet
Will you come back once more, and stand
  Once more beside me, Sweet,
And here again I kiss your hand
  And here again your feet?

SONGS OF THE BELOVED.

I.

ONE kiss I give my Sweet
   On each of her white feet,
One for her forehead meet,
   And one on either eye;
One for her smile to keep,
And two when she doth weep,
And three when she would sleep
   For lullaby.

Ten for her fingertips,
Three for her dimple-dips,
Two for her pouted lips,
   And one for every sigh;
One for each word she saith,
One for her sweeter breath,
And one more sweet than death,
   Lest she should die.

II.

O I will love you, love you, love you;
   And you will love me, will you not, my
      Sweet,
A little, little? Ah if you loved me
   Only a little, life would be complete.

Ah let me love and pet you, pet you,
   Kiss all your face and neck, my Sweet,
      my Sweet;
O come to me and let me kiss you,
   Pet you all over you from head to feet.

Ah I can only when I kiss you
   Tell you how I do love you, thus complete,
Ah Sweetest, only when I pet you
   Why I do love you, all from head to feet.

III.

"Kiss my eyes, Love, if you love them."
   And the truth in me replies
Through my lips, as I do prove them
   Only true upon thine eyes.

Ah those gold-green orbs, whose heaven
   Far outshines the sunset skies;
In whose deeps, as in a haven,
   All my soul at anchor lies!

Thus I kiss them. Nor in laughter
   Nor in smile the answer flies:
Still the suppliant sense sighs after,
   "If you love them, kiss my eyes."

IV.

One more song of the Belovèd
    On her eyes and lips I write,
Lest my lips go home reprovèd
    Of her eyes to-night.

Upon loving lips I leave it,
    Dewy from the lips above;
Let belovèd eyes receive it
    From the lips they love.

Love's own meaning lips can only
    On the lips of love indite;
Eyes late kissed are never lonely
    Waking in the night.

So that both sleep unreprovèd
    Take from off my lips this long
One last kiss of the Belovèd,
    Sweetest, one more song.

A SONG BETWEEN TWO KISSES.

IF all kiss be sweet as this is,
    And thy songs as well do please,
If indeed thy songs be kisses
    Sing me these.

If all lips were sweet as thine are
    Who with kiss and song for choice
But would find the lip diviner
    Than the voice?

Sweet as kiss is song, but fleeter,
    And who kisses sweet and long
But doth find the kisses sweeter
    Than the song?

When the voice is mute 'tis meet lips
    Should with lips arise and greet:
Song begets not song, but sweet lips
    Wed with sweet.

Song intestate dies, nor merits
    Honour for an empty name,
But the kiss bequeathed inherits
    From the same.

So thy songs be kisses, ring me
    Changes on the constant theme
Such as poets use and sing me
    Songs of dream ;

Songs of night, and day her debtor,
    Songs of labour's shadow, rest,
Songs of good, and songs of better,
    Songs of best ;

Songs of sweet that lurks in sorrow,
    Songs of earnest wrapt in play,
Songs of time that veils to-morrow
    From to-day ;

Songs of music and of laughter,
    Songs of smile for eyes that weep,
Songs of vigil, and thereafter
    Songs of sleep ;

Songs of pledge and songs of pardon
  Sung by dawn to waking flowers,
Songs of greenwood to the garden
  After showers;

Songs of kisses, songs unmovèd
  Heard by fancy fancy-free,
Songs of love, and the Belovèd,
  Songs of thee;

Songs of song that like an ember
  Fades from out thy failing breath,
Song such as one may remember
  Even in death.

A SONG OF ROSY LIPS.

NYMPH, whose rosy lips beguiling
    Greet my kisses still with smiling,
Whence this frugal mind?
Say when kisses are so plenty
Why not answer one in twenty,
    Paying back in kind?

Sweet, I love your smiles, believe me,
But for every one you give me
    Give me kisses ten;
Match me still my laugh with laughter,
Smile, but let the kiss come after
    Ere you smile again.

A SONG OF KISSES.

COME and speak to me, child Kitty,
    Come and sit upon my knee ;
Head upon my bosom, Pretty,
    Pressed as lightly as may be,
Whisper me and tell me this,
Kitty, how does Kitty kiss?

Kitty kisses not as others
    Cold and slow but quick and kind ;
Every kiss that follows smothers
    Every one it left behind ;
And the last of that full score
Tastes of all that went before.

Kitty's kisses come like shadows
    Rippling over wind-swept corn,
Like the showers on April meadows
    Falling ere the cloud is born,
Like the flowers upon the hill,
Springing how and where they will.

Kitty has a nape and slender,
   Shadowed by her amber hair,
And I make my soul's surrender
   While I kiss the shadow there,
Shadow of the amber grape
Mantling on her velvet nape.

Kitty has a chin and pretty,
   Cool white chin as ever rose
From a warm white throat, that Kitty
   Guards from kisses very close,
But when asked upon my knees
Lets me kiss it as I please.

Why does Kitty let me kiss her?
   She has never told me why.
If she went, she knows I'd miss her;
   I can see it in the shy
Glance, and kisses springing thick;
Kiss me, Kitty, to the quick.

Why do I like to kiss Kitty?
   Ah that is another tale;

Should the night-jar not in pity
   Answer to the nightingale?
Does the linnet cease to sing
When the lark is on the wing?

How would Kitty that I kissed her?
   Even as I kissed her last:
Sister kisses following sister,
   Not too deep nor yet too fast,
Silent, tender, sweet and kind,
Soft as light and warm as wind.

Best, to tell a simple story,
   She would be kissed through her hair,
Where it frames a golden glory
   For her forehead, like a fair
Young moon risen in the mist:
That's how Kitty would be kissed.

Kitty, let me be your pretty,
   Come and sit upon your knee,
Let me play at being Kitty,
   Kitty play at being me;
When I kiss you then, 'tis true,
It is you that kisses you.

So would I sit still and give you
    Kisses without stint or check,
Make you honeycomb and hive you
    Jasmine kisses in your neck,
Jonquil for your eyelids close,
For each dainty ear wild-rose.

For your throat a kiss of apple,
    For your chin a kiss of pear ;
For your riband autumn-maple
    Kisses, mixed with maidenhair ;
For the full cheeks each by each
Kisses nectarine and peach.

Cream-white kiss for arm and shoulder—
    Creamier white were never kissed—
Milk-white kisses for the colder
    Milken white of hand and wrist ;
Ivory for the slender feet
Folded in a kiss complete.

Amber kisses for the twilit
    Forehead meshed in amber hair ;
Violet kisses for each violet
    Velvet vein that mantles there ;

Crimson for the lip that sighs,
Sea-blue for the sapphire eyes.

For the eyebrows kiss brocaded,
   For the eyelash kisses fringed;
For the tresses kisses braided,
   For the ringlets crimped and cringed;
Smocked for dimples, and the while
Puckered into every smile.

Such at sixteen are the pretty
   Flights we fancy, she and I.
As is kissing, so is Kitty,
   Sweetest when none else is by,
And most sweet in that she will
Keep all kisses secret still.

A SONG OF RESERVE.

COME sup upon my brows to-night,
    Thy hunger else forsworn,
But do not surfeit on their white,
    Lest thou shouldst thirst at morn.

The kiss that leaves the lips forbid
    Taints all that do remain ;
Taste, taste the smooth of either lid,
    But leave the purple vein.

As bees that murmur while they sip
    And kissing leave no sting,
Cool, cool thy thirst on either lip,
    But do not drain the spring.

Kiss on the lips, but not between,
    And shun each dimple still,
The fairest prospect to be seen
    Is ever on the hill.

Take, take away those lips of red,
    They do but hunger mine,
But give me back thy brows for bread,
    Myself will bring the wine.

Here from my lips thine own shall learn
    How lightly Love can feed,
That from Desire is to discern
    As flower is from weed:

Love then most sweet when he is coy,
    As is a maid in bed,
Desire that is a wanton boy,
    And eke a beggar bred:

Love's vine that prunèd still grows higher,
    A curtain for thy need,
But like a poppy young Desire
    That straightway runs to seed.

And if thou read'st my thought aright
    That still pursues the theme,
Sleep not within mine arms to-night
    But only in my dream.

A SONG OF ENTREATY.

O KISS me not for kisses' sake,
   Nor for the moon's alone,
But let the moonlight kiss the lake
   And kiss me for mine own.

Ah not that fever kiss, that slips
   Like lightning from the skies,
But that which lingers from the lips
   Like light upon the eyes.

As roseleaf falling in the dusk
   Should lip on eyelids light,
The kiss that mingles with the musk
   The savour of the white.

That thou wilt find them sweet to woo
   As any rose in bed,
I wager here these eyes of blue
   Against those lips of red.

A SONG OF LOVE.

AH why should eyes for lips' espial
    Unguarded answer bliss for bliss,
Till envy ends his armistice
And lips like eyes take no denial?
Like to the sunbeam on the dial
    That leaves no print of hit or miss,
True love doth make mistakes on trial,
    But pays each forfeit with a kiss.

Ah why doth moonshine, that discovers
    The tricks and trades that ply by night,
Set all her beacon-fires afright
About the fairyland of lovers?
If not that love, the cloud that hovers
    To screen the lips of young delight,
Should spread his pinion like the plover's
    To lure her on to her despite.

Ah why should lips in rapture meeting,
   Their famine turned to plenty, prey,
   And sweetness turned to surfeit, stay,
For kisses kisses still entreating?
Love, growing boy, must still be eating,
   And fill his satchel while he may;
He bakes them in the moonlight, Sweeting,
   For feasting at the peep of day.

A SONG OF FAREWELL.

SWEET heart, our journey ends.
    We part good friends,
Who met in kindly wise, but did not
    know
Of kindlier in that night of sweet mis-
    chance
And snow.
I scarcely loved you then ;
You know we scarcely knew each other
    when
We came from France.

To me you seemed a slip of dawn
Upon the snow,
But shy as any fawn
That ever fed upon a forest lawn
Of Fontainebleau,
Or ran
In Michigan.

I said within myself, "Her heart
Is stolen : it is with the bees
That make a noise among the western
　　trees ;
I have no part
In these."
Yes, it is with the prairie breeze
That wafts his kisses upon mouth and
　　eyes,
And children stealing out upon her with
　　surprise
To kneel upon her knees,
And play about her as in mountain-
　　brooks the showers,
Or yellow butterflies among the yellow
　　flowers.

She comes from out a riper spring than
　　theirs ;
She knows the summer and the failing
　　rains ;
And if a weary heart complains
She takes him to her, and she wears
His sorrow for her sorrow, till he sees it
　　and refrains
From grieving, lest he grieve the love she
　　bears.

She is not all in Italy nor yet among the bees,
The homelight and her darling faces;
She stands like one at sundown in strange reedy places,
And looking sunward, westward o'er the leas.
Strange faces westward! cherubs in the sun,
And flaming images!
But if among the sedge and tangled growth
She finds a weary bird, she is not loath
To stoop and take it in her hands—
The light still strong within her eyes from other lands—
And, maimed, to lay it in her bosom, for she understands;
She has a heart for both.

Dear Love, you have been with me in the dusk
Of grey cathedrals; standing there,
We have outfaced the blazon and the glare
Of crimson window, and the musk
Of scattering censers, and the blare
Of quaking organ, while the stream-light broke,

And fed on every martyred lip the prayer
   that stole,
And lit on every head the aureole;
Or lingering shadow, falling, quenched the
   whole,
And waves of deep sound, rolling sheer
From pier to pier,
Through twilight into twilight rose, from
   gloom to gloom
And fell, a gathering silence, in the doom
Of music felt but heard not, unexpressed
   for fear.

We two have wandered down the length
Of chambers sacred with the life
And solemn with the colour-strength
Of those in subtle guise
Who saw the world within the world of
   the eyes,
The gloom, the majesty, the glow—
The strife
Of Tintoret, Titian the wise,
And Fra Angelico.

Yet though for me
Within this Italy of ours

There are three cities and but three,
Rome of the towers,
And breezy Florence called of flowers,
And Venice of the sea,
I should not choose to have you there,
But out from these, no matter where,
And in or out of broad sunshine,
So you should sit by me, your hand in mine.
The day should be a livelong day
As on the May
When, we two sitting hand in hand,
Our feet were guided through the land.
The curtain fluttered in its place,
The wind was warm upon your face,
And red the morning poppy blew,
The vetches out upon us flew
Among the youngling corn and grew
Before us. For all you had a mind,
The cattle drifting far behind,
The hedges, wild-flowers, and the wind.
I loved you then,
And better than in any other kind
And pride of circumstance ;
And you, I think you did not love me less than when
We came from France.

Venice. 1876.

A SONG OF THE SEA.

FAR above the water's gleaming
    When the sun shines on the bay,
Where even the sea-birds hush their
    screaming,
Overborne by the wind and blown away,
There it stands, a battered bower:
It is called Our Lady's Tower.

There are nobler forts in life
Than this ruin in mid-air;
But none that fronts so dauntlessly the seas,
And rubbing shoulders with the breeze.
If the wind were King of Fife
And Maid Marion were there,
All her hair about her blown,
The wind would take it for his throne;
He would come when flowers are rife
And take Maid Marion to wife.

Ah the wind has many a dove
In the secrets of the cliff:
He is but a light-of-love.
Gazing seaward on the skiff,

All her throat and forehead bare
Where he kissed her,
She he wins not mounts the stair
Far above the waters' springing.
See her swing her hat in singing!
Till her playmate and her sister
Comes upon her, and they fall
To swaying hands for very light of heart,
And stand on tiptoe while they call
To the sail that skims apart.

It is noontide at the hour
When this old dismantled keep
Looks toward its sister tower
Across the sand-dunes and the deep.
The long long ripple slowly swells
At flood the shingle and the shells.
There are two maidens on a reef,
And stepping to and fro upon the ledge;
One falters, and the other reaches out the
    hand.
The tower of the seaward edge
Looks to the tower oversands;
It cannot come to her relief:
They gleam in alien pools and gloom on
    converse lands,
They cannot meet, these two, nor greet,
    nor understand.

It is ebb : the sea has left the land ;
There are footprints on the strand,
There are tender feet
Toiling in the heaps of shifting sand.
The wind blows it in a screed
Of whirling, whisking blinding sleet.
They make headway : see them down once
    more
By the shoals of salt seaweed.
Ah what laughter ! with what peals
Of thunder crackling at the heels !
Ebbward ! down among the dulse ;
There to see the waters pulse ;
There to see the seaweed dress
Her tresses in the sea's caress ;
One may come on star-fish, two and three,
Stark and dreaming of the deep ;
By the lone sea-pools will sleep
The blood-red of the sea-anemone ;
And there is evermore the Sea !
The limpid, liquid, lazy, lisping Sea,
The angry, hungry, thundering, boiling,
    brawling Sea,
The dead and dread and drear and melan-
    choly Sea.

I do not see the faces by moonlight,
They only seem to come in waking day.

The moon shines where I sit and write;
I think to sleep . . . the moon comes
    white,
And so . . . and so . . . the still hours slip
    away:
We sit together far into the night.
But thus it is that when from here
I wish to trace the figures clear,
I turn toward the noonday hour,
And find them in the mouldered tower.

A chime
From the seabord gives the noonday tone.
One is faintly beating time
With a light foot, one is still,
Musing on the seaward sill;
A seamew hovers round at will.
Finding all so much alone,
I take a look around the place
To note if it is still the same:
The solid gray embrasured frame,
The glimpses of blue buoyant space,
The crumbling lime, the random scrawl
In fresco high upon the wall,
The chimney, wind-swept sense and all.
And as I sally out from thence,
They look such children in their seat,

A prompting comes, I know not whence:
"Children, have ye aught to eat?"

Upon a mountain slope I know a wood,
A place of shade and endless solitude.
And there from mossy steeps
The wild strawberry leaps
With hanging stem,
The pitted strawberry peeps,
In heaps and heaps and heaps;
There is no end of them.
I gather out from these a goodly few
And bring to you;
And each upon his leaf the silvern sweet,
As on a woodland winding-sheet.
The wind he dare not stir them for his life,
Nor any king of winds, or king of Fife!
And so I leave them at your feet.
                         Faido. 1876.

A SONG OF SYMPATHY.

LET it not vex thee for a face
  Among the shadows, and a buried
    trust ;
Let it not vex thee, though no breathing-
  space
Be found wherein the shadow shall not sit
Like madness on the brain, nor memories
  wild as dust
In sunbeam cease to flit
At morning and at evenfall
And by the walks and by the garden wall ;
Though wistful children gaze and stray
Darkling about the corridors and the
  mellow
Sunlighted casement, missing from their
  day
The play and the playfellow.

Courage ! even for Her sake,
Who watched with thee the night and saw
  the morning break
That found you awfully withdrawn
From one another and from speech,

And looking each at each,
As those who see not, whose wan eyes are
    far
At gaze, on where the morning-star
Has died within the dawn.

Patience! he is not the less yours
That he is one with silence and the hours
That stole him from among the flowers:
The form dissolves, the power endures.
Peace! You would not disown
With any tumult of regret
The child you cherished for your own,
Betray the faith of these faint eyes at
    taking leave?
They might have told you not to grieve,
That did not ask you to forget.

It may be that I do you wrong;
It must be that I do not know,
Who know it only from the song
You sang a little while ago.
But ah to feel the anguish of the lay
We sang at yester eve, not fearing for the
    morrow,
Is ours to-day
Is sorrow within sorrow.

So be it; yet no idle motions part
The loving soul from loving soul,
The broken from the bruisèd life,
Or dare upon the living face to scroll
The legend of the Bleeding Heart :
No, not though myriad deaths were rife.
No marvel that he cannot come to you.
His faith is with him, he would still be
    true
As yon green cedar to the dew ;
His peace is with him, he was drest
As if for slumber when he went away,
And you, who did not grudge the child his
    play,
You would not stir him from his rest?

Cool winds make music for him, and their
    vows
Are precious round his brows;
Our snows
Have no such quiet as his long repose.
So peace! although betimes the eyes
Should gather dewy at moonrise,
And orbs, that were thy love and hers,
Should haunt you from a hundred skies
And glimmer in the beaded furze.
Nay though you roam afield, by snowdrops
    and the grace

Of visionary footsteps on the lawn
Tracking your Darling to his hiding-place,
The magic of his being still
Will move with you, a rainbow on the hill,
A light ascending with the dawn.
He will come to you as the bride
That lately left her mother's and her father's side,
And tells of all her new delight ;
No more, as when you missed him from your sight,
With eyelids lily-drooping, lily-white,
But glorified,
And all your glory be of love and him,
As cherubim and seraphim.

So bring the dress
You loved him best in, and whatever more endears
This time of mourning through the years,
A solemn festival of tears,
And tell of all his loveliness.
Forget the little grave awhile,
The strange distress,
And think on all the wisdom of his smile.

Strathyre. 1877.

A SONG OF THREE.

DEATH, what of Life? Although the
    grave should move,
  Thy silence is of meaning far more rife,
Albeit thou knowest far less than Life of
    Love,
  Death, what is Life.

Life, what of Love? Let all thy perfumed
    breath
  And red lips with white laughter parted
    prove,
Albeit thou knowest no more than Love of
    Death,
  Life, what is Love.

Love, what of Death? With grief and hate
    at strife,
  Anger and fear, thy tear-drop only saith,
Albeit thou knowest far more than Death
    of Life,
  Love, what is Death.

IN a green nook and shady
    The mill-wheel murmurs on;
But ah its love, my lady,
    Our lily flower is gone.

The mill-race sobs, and sobbing
    My own voice seems to chime;
My heart beats thick and throbbing
    The mill-wheel beats in time.

The sound of many waters
    Is joyous on the air,
If she among the daughters,
    My own true love, were there.

The sun goes down to strengthen
    New worlds at eventide,
And all the moments lengthen
    The shadow at my side.

A SONG OF THE MILL.

The mill-wheel hums, and humming
   It murmurs murmurs on :
It said, *Is coming, coming,*
   It says, *Is gone, is gone.*

Is gone? Is gone for ever,
   From hollow, home, and hill,
From wood, and field, and river
   That feeds the foaming mill.

A SONG OF FOUR.

IF Love were strong as Faith is meek,
    Life still would draw an endless breath:
It is because his arm is weak
    Love cannot cope with Death.

If Faith were warm when Life is old,
    Love would not take the grave to wife:
It is because his heart is cold
    That Death has power on Life.

If Life were long as Love is sweet,
    Faith would prove strong as Death doth prove:
It is because his foot is fleet
    That Life plays false to Love.

A SONG OF THE HERMITAGE.

WOO me not, Woodland, from the cell
    Beneath the mystic pine,
Whose odours at the noon dispel
    An incense rich as wine,
For here beneath its shade did dwell
    The maid I wooed for mine.

They laid her dark in yonder dell,
    The last of all her line,
And in her hand a carven shell
    With mystic circles nine,
And at her head *Rose la Pucelle*,
    Called Rose of Engadine.

Ah Sweet, with eyes of the gazelle
    And foot as ivory fine,
The heart whose heaven is in thy spell
    May well a world resign :
What priest of the pure évangel
    May quit the sacred shrine?

The moon will haunt the woodland well,
  The star within it shine,
And here will hang the purple bell
  And here the bramble twine,
But never more by wood or fell
  For me the morn divine.

.

Thy hermit here my beads I tell,
  And make the secret sign,
And wonder why the streamlets swell,
  And why the days decline,
And why no roses are to smell
  So sweet, dear Wood, as thine.

CHANSON DE LA TROP BIEN AIMÉE.

GLOIRE de Dijon, fleur trop vite éclose
  Sous le soleil trop vif de mon espoir,
Qui me te rendra bouton, reine et rose ?

L'amour, c'est donc la mort ? Le beau le noir ?
La poésie des fleurs mêmes la prose ?
La chanson de midi le chant du soir ?

O triste sort ! triste métempsycose,
Qui aux mains de l'amour tout laisse échoir
A l'instant même de l'apothéose !

A SONG OF A DAY.

LOVE me while you may, Sweet,
    Love has but his day,
Sings his one more lay, Sweet,
    Then he flies away.

Larks fly in the spring, Sweet,
    Singing as they spring,
They would never sing, Sweet,
    But upon the wing.

So Love's song is shy, Sweet,
    If he cannot fly,
Even so it dies, Sweet,
    In a loveless sky.

Once we sealed a vow, Sweet,
    Could we find it now
Upon either brow, Sweet,
    Love and I and thou?

Upon either eye, Sweet,
    Seeking far and nigh?
Ah how either's sigh, Sweet,
    Gives that dream the lie.

Was Love sweet to thee, Sweet,
    Sweet to hear and see?
He can never be, Sweet,
    As wert thou to me:

Sweet to need and know, Sweet,
    Now no longer so;
Pay him what we owe, Sweet,
    Pay and let him go.

When his favours pall, Sweet,
    Nectar turns to gall;
Better let it fall, Sweet,
    Bliss and pain and all.

Say him nay or yea, Sweet,
    He will say thee nay;
Golden sky is gray, Sweet,
    Love has had his day.

A SONG FROM AFAR.

I DO not ask you for your love,
　Or seek to kiss your feet,
Nor yet your fan, nor yet your glove,
　Nor anything so sweet.
I do not ask to take your hand,
　Or kneel beside your knee,
Or even bid you understand
　That you are dear to me.

I do not ask you for a smile,
　I do not bid you play,
I do not beg a song to while
　The songless hours away.
I do not ask to be your glass
　That finds you fair to view;
I only ask to see you pass,
　And pass unseen by you.

A SONG OF THE YOUNG MOON.

FOREHEAD of my only Fair,
    Risen on my dream so soon,
And my landscape everywhere
    In the moon ;

Eyes whose summons infinite,
    Searching all the Milky Way,
Finds me here at break of night
    As of day ;

Lips upon whose pasture mute
    The moon's kisses sink like showers,
Paradise of perfumed fruit,
    Perfumed flowers ;

Breasts that forward leaning stilly
    Darkling in my dream disclose
Hanging gardens of the lily
    And the rose ;

Kisses from those hands outspread
   By the rose-tree on the wall,
Gathered white and gathered red,
   Roses all ;

Hands, that with no fear of malice
   Enfold mine and bid them rest,
Each warm palm a solemn chalice
   For each breast ;

As a star to star to-night,
   As the lake in the moonshine,
Is thy soul in the moonlight
   Unto mine.

What to thee are cloud and calm?
   What of night and her abyss,
Fondled by the tender palm,
   Pilgrim's kiss?

What of moon and what of skies,
   Flown beyond thee and thy ken,
Kissed upon the dreamy eyes,
   Dreamier then?

What of morning and thy vows
   Of a vigil sworn to keep,
Here across my very brows
   Fallen asleep?

Sister, I who here, thy brother,
   Kiss thee only through thy hair,
And had else given many another
   And to spare—

For the starlight on the lake,
   For the lake the star controls,
Kisses for the body's sake
   And the soul's,

For the mute and mystic lands
   Where the moonset lingers still—
Lay this kiss between thy hands
   On the sill:

One, but one, for that lone light,
   And the dawn that draweth nigh,
And for very last good-night
   And good-bye.

A SONG OF THE DREAMLESS LAND.

O DO not say my love is blind,
   If at the banks of yon dark stream
Where sleep parts loving mind from mind
   I cannot dream.

O deem it not the less devout
   Because it does not always sing,
And like a child is wearied out
   At evening.

Love has his golden right of way
   Along the paths no dreams pursue :
My sleep is dreamless, for all day
   I dream of you.

A SONG OF A CHRISTMAS ROSE.

ROSE, that winter's sweet art
    Sprung beneath her feet art,
Let me pluck thee for my Sweetheart
    Here between the snows;
Risen from a far land,
As if fallen from star-land,
All to make a Christmas garland
    For my Christmas Rose.

Winter's Rose and lone love,
First and scarcely blown love,
Here I give thee for my own Love
    This ... and this ... and this ...
Only hoar-drops listen,
Hold their breath and glisten,
While we Christmas' self re-christen
    With a Christmas kiss.

Pines and eve invoke us,
Skies of pearl and crocus,
Frosty light in magic focus
  Round us and above :
Rich the year that closes
As her summer posies,
If she brings with Christmas roses
  Rose of Christmas love.

ENVOI.

PURE heart, that art as perfect rose
　　As I confessed believer,
Whose moonlit beauty warmer glows,
Whose very shadow brighter shows
　　Than sunrise on the river;
Since I do know you not of those
Who scorn the simples love bestows,
Here take my blossom as it blows
　　And kiss it for the giver.

Who claims of right what freedom owes
　　With friendship soon must sever;
The weary heart will end its woes,
The wistful soul will find repose,
　　The wayward seld or never;
And froward comes and fickle goes,
And wilful reaps as wanton sows,
But true love blossoms from the snows
　　A Christmas rose for ever.

A SONG OF THE LAKE.

LOOK, look, the star! One silver ray
    Lies low upon the mere.
Hark, hark, the music from the bay
    How sweet, how clear!

O answer, answer, while the oar
    Drips on the starlit track,
And echoed, echoed from the shore
    The song comes back.

Pull, pull! Like dream the bay, the shoal,
    The bluff, the bank, are past,
And hand in hand, and soul with soul,
    Meet, meet at last.

Sing, sing! Hush, hush! The sleeping mere
    Is silent to the star;
Why waken, now our souls are here,
    Our songs afar?

A SONG OF THE SANDS.

WHEN waves lie down to kiss the sand
    And half the pier is drenched in
        spray,
Come, Children, let us all take hand
    And dance until the break of day.
Maiden with boy, and boy with maid,
    Let all take hold of sunburnt hands,
Fling by the bucket and the spade,
    And dance till sundown on the sands.

The billows hand in hand advance
    On either side along the bay,
They bow, then curtsey, ere they dance
    And dash themselves in foam away.
So bow and curtsey, boys and girls,
    And foot the fairyland you seek,
The breeze blows promise through your
        curls
    And brings fulfilment to each cheek.

The fishing village with its tiles
  Brightens the iris of the sea,
They are not rosier than your smiles
  Nor bluer than your eyes will be.
O let the seaman hug the seas,
  And breast the wave, and brunt the spray
We dream ourselves into the breeze,
  And dance for ever and a day.

CHANSON SANS PAROLES.

SI je t'aime, oui ou non,
    Je ne dirai mot :
J'en sais bien plus long,
    Dis-le, toi, tantôt.

Si tu m'aimes, non ou oui,
    N'est guère à douter :
Moi, je te l'ai dit
    Entre deux baisers.

A SONG OF A VOICE.

HUSH! Whence the music of that note
    That like a fountain springs?
Ah listen to that tender throat!
    Who is it, what, that sings?

O soul, whose cadences are stirred
    To songs from far away,
O voice, whose note at morning heard
    Makes music through the day;

O glowing throat, O golden bird
    From out no silver cage,
Whose strain in every raptured word
    Brings back the golden age:

Sing of the days when time was gay
    And love and I were young,
O let me listen to thy lay,
    And leave my own unsung.

A SONG TO THE SINGER.

SISTER, the song that wakes in thee
    Hath in it forecast of the Spring,
What time the sunny breezes swing
The daffodil beneath the tree:
I seem to sit beside the sea
    And hear a spirit in thee sing.

Thy voice makes many a pleasant place
    To rest in, many a fragrant spot;
    Sweet eyes of the forget-me-not,
The charm of wistful-playful ways,
Bring back a hundred yesterdays
    Of song that may not be forgot.

If at an hour when storm-winds sway
    The clouds through heaven from pole to
        pole,
The passion in thee soars to roll
In music to the Far-away,
Listen within thyself and say
    "It is the Soul, it is the Soul."

A SONG OF COURAGE.

FRIEND, whose honest laughter
    Makes the rooftree ring
And the whole night after
    Sing,

You, whose spirits tandem
    Drive dead heats with time,
Moralise this random
    Rhyme :

Up and make thee merry
    While the wine is red,
And let dead men bury
    Dead.

He who weeps for mischance,
    Save he mend endeavour,
Shall discover his chance
    Never.

All the ages show it,
  All the sages show,
Painter, Singer, Poet
  Know

His own way who carveth
  Is the man who rules :
Hunger only starveth
  Fools.

Not for love of glory
  Sweat thy hour at noon ;
Thou shalt live in story
  Soon.

Morning for tuition,
  Noon for work and will,
Evening for fruition
  Still.

In an hour at farthest
  Thou shalt see it come :
Autumn brings her harvest
  Home.

A SONG OF RHYMES.

AFTER song comes supper
After saddle crupper :
After Solomon comes Tupper.

After saint comes siren,
After silver iron :
After Tennyson comes Byron.

After Tom comes Tonson,
After steamboat sponson :
After Shakespeare comes Ben Jonson.

Before pill physician,
Before cause condition :
Before Tintoret came Titian.

After chicks come chickens,
After thin men thick uns :
After Walter Scott comes Dickens.

Before rosebeds roses,
Before nosegays noses:
Before Montesquieu came Moses.

After boot comes buskin,
After dust the dustbin:
After Adam Smith comes Ruskin.

After shank comes spindle,
After dinner dwindle:
After Faraday comes Tyndall.

After Celt comes Teuton,
After Leghorn Luton:
Leibnitz after Isaac Newton.

After crime comes treason,
But before rhyme reason:
Hence I stop my song in season.

SONGS OF SYMBOLS.

ON AN INVITATION.

WIFE willing, and Self sober, *oui!*
    Yours truly, D.V.
                   D.T.

For V unlimited, my hero,
Means D.T's spirits sunk to zero.
Hence, since one's Wife's one's flesh, bespeak
Flesh willing, but the spirit weak.
Yet . . . " letter kills, spirit gives life."
Then death means living with my Wife ;
For 'tis the *la*tter kills the spirit,
And with it all my wit, or near it.
So off, poor wit, for lack of better,
Lest want of spirit kill the letter.

ON A NEGLECTED DISCOVERER.

PROVE Solomon friend to naked sailors.
    " Take us the $f(o)x$'s, the
      Little dashed—$f(o)x$'s," i.e.
Maclaurin's Theorem. Whence Tailors.

A SONG OF DIFFERENTIALS.

GREAT Nought as *any* other quantity :
   Pure o by o is 1. Calling it "o,"
$$\frac{f(x+o)-f(x)}{o}$$
Is *not*, when o is ze-ro by and by,
$\frac{f(x)-f(x)}{o}$, fie, fie !
   ($\frac{f(x)}{o}$, less self, is o), but lo
$$\frac{f(x+o)-f(x)}{o},$$
dy_x, or as Newton writes, dot-y.

E.g. sin x. $f(x+o)$ is equal
   sin x. cos o + cos x. sin o. Say
   sin x + cos x. o. $f(x)$ away,
Divide by o, and find cos x in sequel.
   The open long-sought secret secretorum
   Of this most elegant Calc. Calculorum.

A SONG OF INTEGRALS.

PRONOUNCE "f-dash." If $\int$, which
pronounce "s,"
But cancels what did dot or d on y,
$y = \int \dot{y}$ identically,
Or $\int f'(x)dx$, as you guess,
If that whole value we may thus express
$\int \frac{dy}{dx} dx$. But why
In this case *both* divide and multiply
By the same term? dx is meaningless.

If *not*, and $\int$ reverse, not dot or d,
But dash or d-by-dx, at the word
$y = y dx$, which is absurd.
And hence there *is* no Diff. Co. nor can be.
Mere points of Form: but which if you
  do see,
Dash f, $d'x$, and go to h for me.

A SONG OF BEAUTY.

BECAUSE of rocks graven by gentlest
    streams,
  Because of tides swayed by the enamoured
    moon,
And of the rose, the maidenhead of June,
Whose thorn deflowers, no bloodless rape
    of dreams ;
Because the sun, whose light, soft as moon-
    beams,
  Lulls all the worlds to slumber like a tune,
  Scorches to fiery heat against the noon ;
Wilt thou find Nature false and in extremes ?

Ask of dread TIME—invisible as Space,
A dream, a symbol, yet holding in command
  All worlds, all gods, all fate, all circumstance,
Omnipotent Nothing, changing changeless
    Face,
Time, of the gossamer foot and iron hand—
  If there be power without elegance.

A SONG OF THE ANTIQUE.

PASS, pass the forms of speech.   Let the
    Form speak :
The small head level as a lance in rest,
Light as a thistle on a meadow-breast,
Severe in contour as the curve is meek ;
The temples delicate, more Greek than Greek—
    To which your Shakespeare's firmamental
      crest
    Was but a chapel monument at best—
The forehead low to crown the oval cheek :

Do these suit better with the signs of class
    And gentle breed—the delicate instant
      nerve,
    High mettle mantling under high reserve—
Than to the subtle workings of the mind ?
Are not all three as one ?   O fool and blind,
Thou that wouldst be more wise than
      Phidias.

A SONG OF POESY.

A TITIAN, sir, a Titian! the flesh-tints
    show it.
Nay, nay, a Beethoven, or else Mozart!
Nay, Verulam! See how thought's
    counterpart,
The form, subdues the thought, and shows
    below it.
Yea, yea, my masters, students, did ye
    know it!
    Though wisdom be of truth the sacred
        heart,
Music the spirit, and colour soul of art,
'Tis wisdom, colour, music, makes the poet.

Down on thy knees adoring at the feet
    Of this most glorious mystic Trinity,
        The WORD made Song, and entering
            into thee
A sacrament of eye and ear, where meet
    The rose, the symbol of all harmony,
The rainbow, vision of the mercy-seat.

A SONG OF THE REVERSE.

TO be crown sycophant, court laureate,
    Flatter the foibles of the purple-bred,
And snivel requiems o'er their pauper dead ;
To muck the royal mews and keep the gate ;
To lead the rising stallion to his mate,
    To fling the slipper at the loveless wed,
    And almost, if not quite, to warm the bed :
Is meed for Some with truth named great in Art ;

But vile in spirit, disloyal, hypocrite.
    Court fool must be court poet, but what rule
Ordains the greatest poet perfect fool ?
Who would be parasite of parasite ?
    Kennel, you slavering hounds, called "men" of letters,
    Or take another thrashing from your betters.

A SONG OF A SONG.

I SING a Song, whose music shall be sung
   On hearths where yet the forest sod is
      green,
  On harvest-fields where only moonbeams
      glean,
When moon and stars are old that now are
      young.
From every bough its psaltery shall be slung,
  And roses wanton in the wires for screen ;
  The humming-bird shall thrill its leaves
      between,
To murmur of the bee its flowers among.

And maids shall wear it on their arm for
      sleeve,
  And glass themselves within its running
      stream,
  And fireflies dance it as a darling dream,
A golden light against the purple eve ;
  And all the dusk and all the woodland
      dim
  Fade like a breath into its dying hymn.

A SONG OF DISCOVERY.

FRET not thyself that, missed on the rebound,
    Some truth doth still elude thee in advance.
    Thought is a reel, and brain a country-dance,
Where truths cross hands, and part, and go the round.
And some foot air, and some the vulgar ground,
    And some are won by craft and some by chance,
    And some begot by art on circumstance,
And some their promise crown, and some confound.

Curse not thy star that thy discovery
    (Experience chief of inexperienced youth)
Is proved thy neighbour's secret by and by,
Some slough of long divined fact, or lie.
    How many an innocent goes to bed with Truth,
And finds her no more maid than he or I.

A SONG OF PASSION.

LOVE comes like light, and goes his
    way in flame ;
  His barb is bloody, if the shaft be white ;
  His lip is sweetness, but no serpent's bite
More poisoned than the kisses of the same.
His scorn is praise, his condescension shame.
  A saint to view, a sinner out of sight,
  A thief by day, a prodigal at night,
His lie is sooth, a pseudonym his name.

Wouldst thou stay Love, then put him to
    the door ;
  To be sworn friend of his thou must offend ;
  To be his enemy, thou must befriend ;
If thou wouldst quit, then call him back
    once more.
  If faith thou needs must keep, deceive
    him well,
Remembering Love's heaven is Faith's hell.

A SONG OF LIGHT-LOVE.

SHE does not find them to her taste,
　　These loves of yours that come and go,
　These fancies—ah too well we know
How fancy runs the heart to waste.
Where light-love breasts the silk in haste,
　　Disdainful of the heel-and-toe,
　　Affection follows fair and slow,
And wins in honour, though outpaced.

Let sentiment play her fancied part,
That takes her artifice for art,
　And join the silks and simpers when
They leave the table where you dine;
But do thou linger with the wine,
　And be a man among the men.

A SONG OF DESIRE.

LUST is love's moon, and shows his face
    at night;
By day he hunts obscure and prowls alone,
Feeding on garbage; he is love's carrion-kite,
    The hound that licks his plate and steals
        his bone.
His fever and his nurse, his toy and scourge,
    Love's man-at-arms and bloodiest foeman
        he;
His sting and antidote, his meat, his purge,
    His hunger, thirst, and his satiety.

If lust by love be fed, count it for ill,
    The shower should feed the brook, not
        brook the shower;
If love by lust, let famine take his fill,
    Lust is the dust that raises love the flower.
But as is flower to flower and dust to dust,
Even so is love still love and lust but lust.

A SONG OF THE EYES.

IT fell upon a day my Heart and I
   Drew toward kissing. First I kissed her
     cheek,
Then would I kiss her eyes, and, sweet and
     shy,
   She turned them to me, though she did
     not speak.
" Ah Love," I said, " it is your eyes that
     kill."
   She blushed, and, with her lips half smile
     half pout,
Made answer, knowing I had kissed my fill,
   " And that is why you fain would put
     them out."

O woman's answer, worthy woman's wit!
   O wit and sweetness in a lip that lies!
O lip and wit and woman, only fit
   To kiss and to be kissed! Put out thine
     eyes?
Ah Love, that knowest I would not if I could,
And I, that know I could not if I would!

A SONG OF PARTS OF SPEECH.

WHY should we speak ; is kissing not enough ?
When lips meet close as ours how can we speak ?
For the words said in kisses, speech is too rough :
Lips unto air are not as lips to cheek,
Far less as lips to lips. Could we both speak and kiss,
That were the sweetest. Then let us, Sweetest, pray,
Speak, kiss, and speak. Yet no, what is amiss?
"Kiss, speak, and kiss," that is what you would say !

And from your lips I read your meaning right,
For still you answer with a kiss. Ah thus,
And not by words, love keeps his secrets tight :
We must be understood of none but us.
So let us, Sweet, speak, question and reply,
Only in kisses you, in kisses I.

A SONG OF THE OPERA.

SALVE dimora! Vow the song a cheat,
   The music coarse, the tenor stale and loud,
  The while we fend a pathway through the crowd
  And find your chariot listening in the street.
  While midnight doffs her mantle of blood-heat
   I take my place, a lover shy and proud,
   Half hid behind that white and scarlet cloud,
  A true Faust by a real Marguerite.

The traffic roars; the carriage glows and whirls
A wanton westward from the fevered east,
  While pleasure drains her lees and mulls her browst.
Safe for one casket hour of hours at least,
Lay your sweet hand in mine, that pearl of pearls,
  A fairer Marguerite by a purer Faust.

A SONG OF HAND IN HAND.

GIVE me your hand again : let it lie close
   In mine, as ever fondling lovers lay
Who sighed for night and blushed to find
   it day,
Close as the perfume shut within the rose.
Ah dear gloved hand! The carriage lamp-
   light glows
  On crowd and thoroughfare and dim cross-
   way.
    Sweet, clasp my wrist and fingers, Sweet,
     I say!
This hour may never come again, who
   knows?

Over your slender hand the scarlet cloak
Is as a red rose—yes, take off your glove—
   Is as a red rose shadowing a white.
Quick, quick, your hand! Ah the swift
   pulse's stroke
Of that warm tender wrist! Ah Love, ah
   Love,
   That quivering palm! What, what, so
     soon? Good-night.

A SONG OF CHANGE.

YOU will not find me if you wait for me
   In the old paths at the old eventide ;
My life has looked upon eternity
   Since last we came along them side by side.
When I did love you late I was a boy,
   And you a girl, whose thoughts were far astray ;
Your eyes were cold, your touch was more than coy,
   And so I wandered too and lost my way.

But when we stood hand clasped in hand to-night
   I was no longer boy ; are you surprised ?
My love has grown from child to manhood's height
   Since in the chalice of your lips baptised :
A love less of divine but more of human,
Because you are no angel but a woman.

A SONG OF SELF-POSSESSION.

SINCE by thy steps I measure out my pace,
   And frame my prospect as thine eyes direct,
I will not sun my love in public ways,
   Nor fan a flame that is not circumspect ;
But stunt my worship, starve my longing sense,
   My looks in prison put, my lips in pawn,
Not raze the shoot, but bind it within fence,
   Not quench the light, but keep the curtain drawn.

So for dear love's sake, I my love repress,
   The more insatiate prudent still the more ;
Yet not too prudent, less the world should guess
   What She I wish to seem not to adore.
Thyself would wish only thyself should know
To judge me by my thought and not by show.

A SONG OF HEED.

YOU will not leave his protest half un-
        heard,
    Nor take a gentle lover's mind amiss,
    Whose only and whose venial fault it is
He dare not lightly take your lightest word.
If you say Stay, why then he means to stay,
    If you say Go, he cannot choose but go,
    If you say Come, why then it shall be so
At his dear Mistress' bidding night or day.

Only, no purpose betwixt hope and fear,
    No pact divided, no unguarded vows;
    That still love's first performance may be
        spouse
To his last promise, though it cost him dear.
    Let no compunction cross the willing mind:
    You must be constant, if you would be kind.

A SONG OF NAMES.

FIVE names you have: the first for charity,
Virtue and tender healing; the next for spirit
And playfulness; the rest for courtesy,
Endurance, dignity. Yet such your merit
Not all of these may half express the human
The divine Being that at your birth took breath,
The Woman here that is far more of woman
Than all of these say or than any saith.

What is my name for you? I have not any;
A thousand in your circle would not meet.
Nay, if I come to choose, I have too many,
Dearest, Belovèd, Ownest, Darling, Sweet.
I have a thousand thousand names for thee,
Then by what one shouldst thou be known to me?

A SONG OF THE FOURTH COMMANDMENT.

SPOILT Child, here is thy Collect. Did I vow
  The Sabbath was thy day, and did not keep it
Holy to thy sweet ordinance? O do thou
  Pardon a first love's first transgression, sweep it
From thy remembrance: for I vow and swear
  I would keep all days holy unto thee,
Who count each moment lost beyond despair
  That is not steeped in thy idolatry.

Yea, I will keep thy Sabbaths and thy laws,
  Thy moons and feasts, so thou be reconciled.
Thyself art my commandment, and with cause:
  I have no other God but thee, sweet Child.
So read me as I write, and find it true,
The day's Epistle is its Gospel too.

A SONG OF DEFIANCE.

YES, I will kiss your dress, you shall not
    stay me.
Keep still, I say you shall not. Who are
    you,
That you should not be worshipped? Nay
    gainsay me,
And I will lift the hem and kiss that too.
You to my face, you dare to tell me this,
    I am so far, far far too far, above you,
Whose only vantage over you it is,
    Whose one diviner feature, that I love you.

What, do you think I boast? Nay then, I
    pray you,
    Let me retain the single grace I have.
In everything but this I would obey you:
    I am no tyrant, Lady, yet no slave.
Take back that insult! What, would you
    repeat
An outrage to your lover at your feet?

CHANSON DE DÉFI.

À NOUS deux, maintenant! j'enrage...
　　J'en suis bien las! de ma constance,
De toi, et de ta nonchalance,
Toujours chagrin, toujours chantage!
À nous! que le duel s'engage!
　　Et pour défi en permanence
　　Voilà mon baiser de vengeance
Comme un soufflet en plein visage!

Je n'en peux plus! mon cœur s'élance...
　　En garde! il y va de la vie!
　　La Foi contre la Tyrannie,
Et toi la Prusse, et moi la France!
À nous deux! duel à outrance!
　　Puis que... je t'aime à la folie!

A SONG OF SOLICITUDE.

AH had I known, my Sweet, my perfect Sweet,
  'Twas you that felt, no torrent and no rain,
No seas had drowned, nor iciest cruel sleet
  Chilled in mine ears that cry of human pain.
But you are used to it! Used, used to what?
Neglect as bitter as these tears of brine,
Suspense sore as thy sighs ; but not, say not
  From wilfulness or apathy of mine?

Too well you know how in long seasons since
  Love played the marksman with my heart for tree :
Your bow it was that shot his arrows thence ;
  And shall they now fly back to you from me?
Weep not, lest after all my sorrow prove
Not that you love me not, but that you love.

A SONG OF CROSS-PURPOSE.

IF you, dear Friend, had earlier divined
   We were no more than friends, and must remain
As had the roses never intertwined
   Nor passion dwelt embowered above us twain ;
If in his summer fancy would consent
   To roam a butterfly and not the bee,
Or linger in the orchard well content
   To lift the fallen pear not shake the tree :

We might keep friendship whole and love to boot.
   Yet here our fortune with his dalliance ends :
He grafts his promise on a barren shoot,
   We are not lovers, and so are not friends.
Our purpose still is with false purpose crossed,
And even for love's sake love is well nigh lost.

A SONG OF PARTING.

GOOD-NIGHT, good-night ! How, then,
  is the night good,
That, holding welcome at arm's length in
    space,
Stifles farewell in his most loathed embrace,
Farewell that would be welcome if it could ?
Even as the sombre aisles of the fir-wood
  Paint the pale peak with purple and the
    grace
Of vanished dawn : even as the sweetest face
Is sweeter darkling kissed, and 'neath the hood.

O kiss most sweet ! • Then let me kiss the
    night,
  That makes farewell so welcome-sweet as
    this.
  O night most sweet ! Then will I kiss
    the kiss,
That makes the night a day-dream for de-
    light.
  Good-night, sweet kiss ! lest, spite of night
    and will,
  Good-morrow find us here, and kissing still.

A SONG OF BEQUEST.

NOTHING I leave thee sweeter than this
    kiss,
  To be thy staff and scrip, thy food and
    clothing ;
  And, take it or in liking or in loathing,
Thou wilt not find another such as this.
It was my all : thy gain is my amiss,
  Sans bed, sans salve, sans seal of my be-
    trothing,
  Content to give thee all and call it
    nothing,
So thou but find it sweeter than it is.

And wilt thou then take all, O beauteous
    born,
  A beggar at Love's door, this moment
    even
  Of charity exalted into heaven,
And leave him here a torment and a scorn,
  Thy Dives more accurst ? Sweet Lazarus,
  Even from Love's bosom look down on
    Tantalus.

A SONG OF COMPARISON.

MINGLE the legends: talk of Hercules
    And all his labours; of Enceladus,
The Babel-builders, Samson, Sisyphus;
Earth's wars and woes, her Iliads, Odysseys;
Of Jonah, Jason and his Chersonese;
    Of Cain, Prometheus, Uzzah, Icarus;
    Of Job, Laocoon and Oedipus;
Oenone's sorrows, Rizpah's, Niobe's;

Tell of all nature's torments toils and throes,
    That freeze for fear the torrents on the steep,
    That turn the rocks to eyes and make them weep,
And add all women's and all men's to those:
    Then find the tale a mocking-bird's, a dove's,
    A myth, a dream, a jest, a lie, to Love's.

A SONG OF REVERSION.

FIRST kiss, first smart : dear pleasure,
worst annoy,
Who would keep faith with love, if love
be pain?
Not I, i' faith. Come back, my kiss,
again !
If sweet be sour, what wonder love is coy?
He sat awhile and wept, the beauteous boy,
To see his roses pale, his morning wane,
The cloud that shows the rainbow sheds
the rain,
And grief is dearest bought when bought
with joy.

First love, first pain : and yet within the hour
Doth pain return to love to heal the
smart ;
As dew that seeks the sun converts to
shower,
Bliss—pain—and—bliss is cycle of the heart.
Avaunt then, kiss, if lips but part to meet,
Let sweet turn sour, since sad returns to
sweet.

A SONG OF THE SOUTHWEST WIND.

O WILD wet Southwest Wind in wild wet showers
   Blown all day from the wet wild western sea
Straight from thy home to hers among the bowers,
   Take this swift message to my Heart from me.
Tell her her beauty will be voiced and sung
   In farther lands than thou shalt ever find,
Tell her her praises will be fresh and young
   When all things else are old and out of mind.

Whisper thou canst not, murmur dost not dare,
   So shout thy message till her ears burn red ;
Weary her eyes, shake loose her robe, her hair,
   Blow out the light and bear her into bed.
Be to her amorous, be to her kind,
   Spite of thy showers, O wild wet Southwest Wind.

A SONG OF THE VINTAGE.

I PLEDGE thee not in draughts of still-born Rhine,
  Nor that which mantles amber in the bell,
  Foam rampant to the brim of broad Moselle,
But in the bath of thy dear charms divine.
Come forth, O Aphrodite from the brine,
  Thy hair yet pregnant with its taste and smell,
  Thy breasts pineapples drowsed with Muscatel,
Thy lips wild strawberries steeped in Tuscan wine.

Come forth from that warm bath as from a bed
  Spiced with the musk of thee, that I may lie
  And drink it in at brow and breast and eye,
Its white wine seething up amid the red.
Come forth, O thou, even from among the dead,
  That I may drink my fill of thee, and die!

A SONG OF THE WARDROBE.

AND I will write my song within thine
    eyes,
And in each silken curl a verse entwine,
And on thy bosom shall its head recline,
And to thy breath its music fall and rise.
And it shall swathe thy beauty fold by fold,
    And fit to every finger like a glove,
    Thy sandals broidered scarlet with its love,
Thy spirit, like thy raiment, breathing gold.

Earth shall be clad from thee, as is the
    Night,
    The Day's handmaiden, from the spoils
      of Day,
    And Day and Night, thy sempstresses, array
Thy mysteries in fresh glamour of delight;
    While even in thy dreams shall Sleep
      rehearse
Unto the worlds the glory of my verse.

A SONG OF THE BEDCHAMBER.

WHEN all in white I picture thee arrayed
As if for sleep, thy vestal beauty warm
In the cool robe that mocks the breathing form,
When thus I dream, Sweet, I would be thy maid,
Lay by thy festal raiment, tire thy hair,
 Thy nymphs my fingers, talk to thee the while,
 And with my hand upon the door would smile
Good-night, sweet Mistress, and so down the stair.

Ah let me be thy wardrobe, Sweet, thy bed!
 Ah Sweet, I would be anything of thee,
 Thy scarf, thy glove, thy glass, thy jewelry,
Thy coverlet, the pillow for thine head.
 And if it were the grave where thou dost lie,
 Dear Sweet, I would lie down in it and die.

A SONG TO BEDWARD.

TO bed, to bed, O weary head and breast!
    Dew with the eve, and dewy sleep for pain,
Deep dreamless sleep for sick of heart and brain :
Even for the weary cometh sometime rest.
Calm with the moon, and slumber in the west,
    A cloudland soft as moonrise come again :
Sleep, parchèd lip, the night shall bring thee rain,
Sleep, fitful fiery pulse, for sleep is best.

Rest, aching eyes, too weary even to weep,
Rest, throbbing brows, for even pain must sleep ;
    Fold, wan worn limbs, and pillow, restless head,
A calm more sweet than dream, more deep than death ;
Hush, fevered moan, to waken balmy breath,
    Sleep, sighs, and waken smiles. To bed, to bed.

A SONG OF SOLITUDE.

To have loved only once : to have been fed
    A mountain lake by the one secret
        stream ;
A dreamer, tossing on his fevered bed,
    Who turns at morning to the selfsame
        dream ;
A bird that builds her every year her nest
    Within the shelter of the same dark bough ;
An infant groping for the same dear breast,
    A mother kissing the same still-born brow :

This is my fate, to have been and to be
    A music thrilling to the one sweet tune,
A moon that looks on the same changeful sea,
    A sea still turned to the same constant
        moon :
This is my fate, O tender spirit and true,
To have loved only once, to have loved You.

SONGS OF THE EARLY DEAD.

I.

YOU will not live long, will you not? why
   not?
What ails you at the face of sea and sky?
Why should my Swallow be the first to fly,
And so sweet music be so soon forgot?
Must Love indeed come pilgrim to the spot
   Where limbs once swift to speed to him do
      lie?
Shall vassal Death be sovereign of your lot,
And fall in love with you as well as I?

Will you go to him as to a bridegroom,
   And give the kisses you withheld from me,
His slave and mistress in the bridal gloom?
   Shall you be bound to him, and I be free?
Nay, do not fear him, let him do his worst:
Death may take me, if thou shalt have died
   first.

II.

Soft : who mourns the early dead
   Doth but play the mime to pain,
   If with bitter tears he stain
That green covering of each head.
Morn, that mourns her roses shed,
   Weeps in mist and not in rain ;
   Rose, that weeps her earliest slain,
Bends in silence o'er the bed.

They whose passing bell hath rung
   Had but withered and grown old
   Even to thee ; now in the mould
Bloom, as thou didst know them, young.
   Spirits dead before their time
   Live for ever in their prime.

III.

Hush : who weeps the spirit fled
   Must not give his sighs the rein,
   Nor with angry sob profane
Sanctuary of the dead.
Solemn lip and eye instead
   Bring as mourners in the train
   Of the sorrowing heart and brain,
Secret foot and silent tread.

In the winter of thy woe
Garb for warmth and not for show:
   Tears that have no help of breath
Fall as still as falling snow.
Let them, Spirit : there are no
   Secrets between Grief and Death.

IV.

Heaven grew to summer in blue laughing
   skies,
  Summer, in one green smile of her train-
   bands,
To one red dream of roses through the lands
Spread like the winding streams of Paradise.
We lingered by their whispering galleries
  In gardens sunshot over golden sands,
  And there, thy face a rose between my
   hands,
I kissed thee like a sunset on the eyes.

But since that Death hath sealed up either eye,
  And bound thy face within his cold white
   band,
  Is heaven fled from earth through all the
   land,
And from the heaven the sky, and from the sky
  Her blue, and from the very rose her red ;
  And all the world may die, now thou art
   dead.

V.

I fashioned me a world of passing rare:
  And there was Autumn with her golden
      bough,
  And Summer with her roses at the prow,
And Springtide with her hawthorn in the air;
And Noonday with her cloth-of-gold for wear,
  And Midnight with her hand upon the
      Plough,
  And Evening with the star upon her brow,
And Morning with the rainbow in her hair.

I fashioned Sleep with feet and bosom bare,
  And thee asleep, and still had kept my vow
That only Sleep and I should find thee fair,
Had not foul Death—ah traitor Death, where,
    where
  Is he that I may slay him?—forestalled me
    now.
  Where, where is Death? Ah Love, and
    where art thou?

A SONG OF INTERSPACE.

THOU art my planet and no fixèd star,
    O glory hidden in the light of noon,
Though I did seek thee late and find thee far,
    More cold and more inconstant than the
        moon.
My love my glass, I looked and I divined
    Thy orb majestic and more pure than gold,
Its light as constant still as it was kind,
    And kindlier even than I thought it cold.

Yet art thou far : found found alas too late,
    And worshipped only for a mystic light,
Night's countercharm, the counterpoise of
        fate ;
    Even as that star in yonder infinite,
Moving a world apart, unnamed, unknown,
    And loved for its eternity alone.

A SONG OF SONGS.

SONGS of thee I give thee, giving
    All the best of me,
Leave with thee my sweetest, leaving
    Songs of thee :

Some that fly far out to sea,
    Some, despite their striving,
Backward blown from wind to lee :

All in fancy ways contriving
    Theeward as they flee,
Dreams and fancies all but living
    Songs of thee.

SONGS OF SONG.

I.

EINST geliebt, die frohen Lieder
  Die die Liebesgluth eingibt
Leg' ich dir zu Füssen nieder
Einst geliebt.

An das Herz, das nur aufschiebt
Nicht versagt, nimm du sie wieder
Schuldlos dessen ich verübt:

Nicht, wie sonst, zerstreute Glieder
Eines Opfers gar betrübt,
Sondern eins gewordene Brüder
Einst geliebt.

II.

Set in our songs one word
That unto thee belongs,
Thy Name, Beloved, Adored,
    Set in our songs.

One music fullest throngs
The senses, never stirred
To trumpets, cymbals, gongs :

One anthem, sweetest heard
Sung by familiar tongues :
Thy Name ! that note, that chord
    Set in our songs.

III.

She set her music to the words,
And, when her whiter hand has met
White keys, she sings and strikes the chords
    She set.

Ah at that hour when eyes are wet,
And sorrow, crossing at the fords
Of song the torrent of regret,

Takes all the healing she accords—
Who that has once heard can forget
The more than music in the words
    She set?

IV.

Here at thy feet he sits, and, softly fanned,
The chancel music swells that, strong or
    sweet,
Springs like a fountainhead at thy com-
    mand
      Here at thy feet.

Music and song together rise and beat
Their wings as one. The pale cheek glows,
    the bland
Eyes melt in light as from a mercy-seat.

And ah what prophet of that painted band,
Hearing and seeing thee, his Paraclete,
What saint or angel of that rainbow land
Would not, descending from his jasper
    street,
Lay all his heavenly honours in thy hand,
      Here at thy feet?

A SONG OF A SMILE.

FAITH keeps the keys of that calm smile,
    And registers its pure decrees,
Secure of watch and warden while
    Faith keeps the keys:

The smile of summer on blue seas
Embracing round a halcyon isle,
A gentle majesty at ease:

No glances guarded to beguile,
Or only gay to taunt and tease,
No absent mockery of a smile:
    Faith keeps the keys.

SONGS OF A PORTRAIT.

I.

GREEN eyes and ruddy hair! Not yonder hue,
O painter to the mode of moon and skies.
Sunburn that harvest gold, and put for blue
    Green eyes.

Tender and loving hand, not loving-wise,
Will you limn false, in hope to find it true,
Patron of solar myths and lunar lies?

Will you turn oculist and perfumer too,
Stale vendor of cheap washes and cheap dyes?
Young Beauty's groom and landscape-gardener you,
    Green eyes!

II.

Paint me no paint! Paint me the things I
    know,
Or be they bright or dark, common or quaint.
For as they are I still would have them. So
    Paint me no paint.

Dip in the inner rainbow's faintest faint
A sunbeam brush, thy golden palette the bow
Of last night's moon, and limn without a taint

A Woman fine as flame and pure as snow,
And so she were no portrait of *my* Saint,
Were she thrice saint I would not have her.
    No!
        Paint me no paint.

A SONG OF DEVOTION.

FOND as is sea of sky, and sky of azure,
    Fond as sick-fancied youth of love-lore
        conned
By moonlight, or as age is of his leisure
    Fond ;

Fond as is grief of every garment donned
For death's sake, merit of meed, and need
    of treasure,
As kisses are of kisses that respond ;

Fond as is sleep of night, and night of pleasure,
Am I of thee : nay fonder far, beyond
All scope, all comprehension, and all measure
    Fond.

A SONG OF LENT.

IT is Love's fast to-day ; no sight, no word
   Of thee, a sky from morning overcast ;
And, hearing and seeing not, I saw and heard
   It is Love's fast.

It must be I am dainty ; that thou hast
Been as a surfeit, the spoilt child in me stirred
To fancying thou art not as thou wast :

And for a distance gay a landscape blurred,
And for life's passing-sweet an overpast,
And for its music here a songless bird :
   It is Love's fast.

SONGS OF ENVOI.

I.

SWEET, as you please: what can I answer more?
Put on your silver sandals, skim the seas,
And show yourself to earth from shore to shore
    Sweet as you please.

On what far isthmus will you take your ease,
What inland or what island famed of yore,
What gardens of what new Hesperides?

Only come back to us as heretofore,
As sweet to touch, to tend, to taste, to tease,
As safe, as soon to loving hearts and sore,
    Sweet, as you please.

II.

My Peace I leave with thee, bequeathing Her
Whose worth increaseth with the days' in-
    crease,
That no plague vex nor idle danger stir
    My Peace.

Let Faith attest the deed, Love frame the
    lease,
To have and hold, as these brief signs aver,
Until the year determine and decease,

Whose lapse restores among the gifts that
    were,
Back from her voyage of the Golden Fleece,
Back from the fields of frankincense and myrrh,
    My Peace.

SONGS OF ABSENCE.

I.

GONE from us the one completest
    Thing our day looks on,
Of our dreams the very sweetest
    Gone.

Morning shines as never shone
    Morning, yet our fleetest
Footstep quits its dews at dawn.

O fond lover, breast that beatest,
    Will not day anon
Bring thee back thy lamb, that bleatest
    "Gone?"

II.

With sick eyes awaking, hollow
As from troubled dreams, I rise,
Seeing all things sad and shallow
　　With sick eyes.

Half the dawn in shadow lies,
Only in the east a sallow
Light divides the earth and skies;

And a bird flies . . . O my Swallow,
Gone from where thy lover sighs,
And can only sigh, and follow
　　With sick eyes!

A SONG OF WELCOME.

HOME and rest, for all this weary weather,
    Bird of morning, faint for night and
        nest,
For the springs, the upper and the nether,
    Home and rest.

Back from who love well to who love best,
Back to me, even me, who know not whether
Here to love or love not be more blest:

Bird of broken wing and drooping feather,
Bird of weary eye and bleeding breast,
Faint in arms of thine to find together
    Home and rest.

A SONG OF RETURN.

SONG has come back with Love, as light
    with morn,
His foot as morning's, gay upon the track:
With cheer for gloom, and smile instead of
    scorn,
    Song has come back.

A churl of late in borrowed garments black,
A spendthrift left in sunless fields forlorn;
Not prodigal to others of thy lack,

But sad, deaf-mute. Ah hear him wind his
    horn,
His beagles clamorous for the swift attack,
His eye like sunshine on the fields of corn:
    Song has come back.

CHANSON DU BAISER PERDU.

*B*AISER perdu, baiser
    Malheureux, méconnu,
Qui vas-tu donc chercher,
    Baiser perdu ?

La reconnaîtrais-tu ?
L'entends-tu pleurnicher
À l'instant à l'affût ?

Vite ! le bien pleuré
N'est guère mal venu :
Allons la consoler,
    Baiser perdu.

SONGS OF THE NEST.

I.

Go, sweet kisses, warm from the nest,
　　Go, since my Sweet will have it so,
Callow fledglings and all the rest,
　　Go.

Feathered white as the foam-flakes blow,
Feathered red as the robin's vest,
All for the love of her, high and low;

Fall on her neck and fall on her breast,
Smother her up in a falling snow;
Each in the way that seemeth him best,
　　Go.

II.

Come back, kisses, at peep of night,
Homing straight as the wild-bees home,
You of the red breast, you of the white,
    Come:

Wakeful all, if wistful some,
Warm from the nest that you leave so light,
Back to the lips that you left but numb :

Blithe from the eyes you have kissed more
    bright,
Home to the nest that hath long been dumb :
Pell-mell all as you took your flight,
    Come.

A SONG OF SWEET LIPS.

SWEET lips, kiss on: quick come-again-
 and-gone
 Soft wild-bee sips,
That sweetlier taste than kisses rained upon
 Sweet lips:

Quick gone-and-come, as in the south wind
 dips
 Wet ivy on
Wet ivy, and the cowering lime-tree drips:

Vague as the music played in unison
 By finger-tips
On dreaming brows: kiss gently, but kiss on,
 Sweet lips.

SONGS OF THE ROSE.

I.

HANG low, sweet Rose, for, Rose,
    My kiss hath far to go:
The roses all that doze
    Hang low.

I strain upon tiptoe:
Bend as the spray that blows
When winds walk to and fro.

Hang white, for lips to close
Like sunset on thy snow;
Hang red, but Rose, sweet Rose,
    Hang low.

II.

To red the sunset burns to-night : how chilly
    The still blue overhead ;
The white of yonder snowpeaks turning stilly
    To red.

It is an hour when soul and sense are wed,
    And white breasts, willy-nilly,
Burn rosier in its kisses sunset-bred :

Burn, while the flush of sunset lingers chilly
    From all but yon snows fled,
And rest, their roses kissed to white, their lily
    To red.

III.

Rosebud of twain, hung for all lips' delight
That live on roses for their mortal food,
O shall I kiss the dark or kiss the bright
    Rosebud?

O silent kiss, of love well understood :
O solemn wild bud, warm in the moonlight,
O wild bud, tasting in the shade as good!

O Rose, what shall I answer to the Night,
Who breathe the very perfume of thy blood,
Kissing the red rosebud all kissed to white
    Rosebud?

IV.

Crowned and blest, the one star of that
    million
That Night wears as jewels on her breast,
Pendant to a heaven of many a billion
    Crowned and blest :

Crowned of one red sapphire kissed to rest
On a cushion soft and white as pillion
Of the cloud at noon twixt east and west.

Rosy as the light that rides postilion
On that cloud at even, she yields my hest,
Scorned of Kedar, but in Love's pavilion
    Crowned and blest.

A SONG OF BEATING HEART.

YOUR heart was it or mine I heard,
    So loudly that it made me start?
What was it fluttered like a bird
    Your heart?

A still pool where twin fishes dart,
A still copse till the pheasant whirred,
Two watches, ticking hard apart,

Each by the other's motion stirred:
O kiss, unconscious of Love's art!
What wonder that my heart-beat spurred
    Your heart?

SONGS OF THE STARLIGHT.

I.

ALL but asleep in the all but bed of
    arms that enfold her,
  Arms that engulf in the night of a
    dreamless deep,
Heart beating fainter, eyes closing wearier,
    lips growing colder,
All but asleep.

Heavy the perfume of tresses that lightly
    loosen and sweep
  Over her neck and her breast from
    shoulder to shoulder ;
What does she reck of Love's moonset or
    moonrise, his springtides or neap ?

What of the embers of passion half-
    quenched that flicker and smoulder,
  Ghosts of the slain of her kisses, heap
    upon heap,
Drugged with the warmth of the lips that
    caress, the limbs that uphold her
All but asleep ?

II.

Orion stayed that night to watch our fond
    farewell,
And all the host of heaven with him
    breathless made
Obeisance at the shrine where far above
    the fell
    Orion stayed.

What of that hour, when eyes of stars that
    had seen fade
Thebes, Ilion, Babel, Nineveh, cast down
    to hell,
Gazed down on stars of eyes that watched
    them undismayed?

What of that dream remains, its secret
    guarded well,
Of eyes to eyes alone, of star to star
    betrayed?
Only our gaze that night, your dreams and
    mine, to tell
    Orion stayed.

A SONG OF PARDON.

THINK not of that sharp word: I have
    forgiven.
Love laughs at sharp and blunt, and sharp
    and flat,
Else is not Love. I will not speak, and even
    Think not, of that.

Whose kiss forgiven came startling like the
    bat
But yester-eve when earth reached up to
    heaven,
And night grew into morning as we sat?

And shall Love shrive, and not herself be
    shriven,
Give alms and starve, taste lean and not
    the fat?
Forgiven seven times? Nay seven times
    seven :
    Think not of that.

A SONG AT BEST.

DEAREST and best, with whom I wage
    War of a passion half in jest,
Sole shrine of all my pilgrimage,
My hemisphere from east to west,
May-garden of the golden age,
   Dearest and best ;

O most sedate when most caressed,
Proud queen to whom my soul is page,
But shy as bird to leave her nest,
Say have you taken for your gage,
Love is not love that is confessed?

You peck my crumbs, serene and sage,
You perch upon my hand and breast,
Sweet pilgrim to love's hermitage,
Dearer and better than the rest,
But will not come into the cage,
   Dearest and best.

A SONG OF DREAMLAND.

PASS by me, Sweet, in dreams, I do not bid
    thee stay ;
Thy fate and mine may never come more
    nigh ;
Even as dreams themselves meet and at the
    cross-way
Pass by.

Not with the tear of pity, lingering step and
    sigh,
Not with untoward smile or laughter gay,
Not with averted head and half-averted eye ;

But like a dream, that passes in the morning-
    gray,
Pure, sweet, and silent, look serene and high ;
And, if it were a dream of night, or dream of
    day,
Pass by.

A SONG OF UNREQUITAL.

WHEN blue eyes fill, and lips are trem-
    bling
With piteous dumb desire, that will
Express itself beyond dissembling
    When blue eyes fill,

Ah who can bid the lips be still,
Or check the bitter tears assembling
For lips a-cold and eyes that chill:

Eyes that to tears give no resembling
Pity, proud lips that only kill
In answer to the red lips trembling
    When blue eyes fill?

A SONG OF THE VANISHED.

FOR ever, faces bright,
   Our sighs may bring back never,
Gone from our dreams, our sight
   For ever.

And this is all endeavour!
Meet, love, kiss, hands unite,
And then take hands and sever:

A dark, a dawn, a light,
A glow, a chill, a fever;
A day, and then the night
   For ever.

SONGS OF DESOLATION.

I.

TOO weak to care : the vacant words must
    fly,
The weary eyes resume the vacant stare,
The vacant mood repeat the weary cry,
    Too weak to care.

Let sunset pour her blood upon the air,
The windlet sue the cloudlet through the sky,
The night count all her worlds and find them
    fair :

What matters morn or eve to such as I,
Whose waking is a dream of one despair,
Whether I dream or wake, or live or die,
    Too weak to care?

II.

Life, like Night, hath spread her solitary sable
    pinion,
  Darkening earth aghast from heaven in her
    flight,
Under seal of Death that holds in brooding
    blind dominion
  Life, like Night.

Astral silence : such as follows storm and
    fight,
Strife of wind and waters, beasts and men ;
    even brute Opinion
  Slumbers, he who roars so loud and sleeps
    so light.

Exultation, as in scorn of Time and Dawn,
    his minion,
  That shall deathless raise his mailèd hand
    and smite
Dead the pulseless beat of Chaos trammelling,
    cog and pinion,
  Life, like Night.

III.

After these years what hostel have I found,
What wine and mead for nights and days of
    tears?
Is this waste wind-scourged land my holy
    ground,
That wild mist-blinded moon the light that
    cheers,
That midnight sky my heaven glory-crowned
    After these years?

I come, not well-come; knock, no light
    appears;
Cry, and no answer hails, my crying drowned
In the wind's; I shake the latch, and no one
    hears.

Why should I longer tarry, hearing the sound
Alone of my own footsteps in my ears;
Seeing my white face in the pane, and wound
About from head to foot in worse than fears;
Pacing for nights to come the same sad round
    After these years?

IV.

Smile on me then when life is of fresh worth,
And women are less cruel cold than men;
When grief slacks rein and courage tightens girth,
    Smile on me then.

The sun, past-master of the heavens, again
Smiles on the moon, kept-mistress of the earth,
Though she have slept her hour beyond his ken.

When night gives place to morning, death to birth,
And love, the heron, rising from his fen
Kneedeep in tears, takes wing for skies of mirth,
    Smile on me then.

V.

Le monde en veut toujours aux gueux.
  Plus on est faible, il l'affaiblit ;
  Plus on est riche, il l'enrichit ;
Moins on a, plus il lui en veut.

Plus on a soif et ventre creux,
  Plus il le laisse inassouvi ;
Plus on est humble et souffreteux,
  Plus il le fourre dans l'oubli.

Moins on est gai et fier et preux,
  Moins on en trouve pour ami ;
  Plus grand des malheurs est ceci
D'être reconnu malheureux.
Le monde en veut toujours aux gueux.

A SONG OF TRUTH.

THOU wilt not find me by the brook,
    Nor in the house, nor yet behind,
Nor up the lane, and if thou look
    Thou wilt not find.

My name is TRUTH. It is the mind
Discerns the form the eyes mistook.
I am not seen, I am divined.

Seek in thyself, that secret nook,
And know, when other sense is blind,
What in the mart, the field, the book
    Thou wilt not find.

SONGS OF THE POETS.

I.

SHAKESPEARE, thy name draws the
    gods from their skies:
With thine appearing worlds on worlds
    appear,
And all creation re-created cries
    "Shakespeare."

Earth's first pole-star of Song, a constant
    sphere,
While other constellations set and rise,
Thy phases seasons of the Poet's year:

To thee their worship and their sacrifice
All times and climes surrender far and near.
Thou hast one name among the Wise, the wise
    Shakespeare.

II.

Wordsworth, the spirit of the lonely fell
Was thine, proud soul and lonely from thy
    birth ;
But thou wast poet of thy kind as well,
    Wordsworth.

Secure in habit, rustic in thy mirth,
The acolyte of wood and lake and dell,
A god in stature, if but man in girth ;

High as a mountain peak thy soul did dwell,
Pure as the mountain air in love with earth,
But deep as mountain tarn : and hence thy
    spell,
    Wordsworth.

III.

Shelley, Swinburne, your soul is as the flame
That strews the zenith with the night's
   return,
Your spirits twin-stars, and like a star each
   name,
     Shelley, Swinburne :

Your song a sun, whose ardorous pulses spurn
Swift surge of music, incensed whence it
   came,
A fire at heart, for all hearts to discern :

Your fame a moon, attendant on the same,
Attended of all eyes, that all may learn
No mist may tarnish and no night may tame
     Shelley, Swinburne.

IV.

Tennyson, thy Muse of old
Shows no art's diviner denizen :
Painter, poet three times told,
    Tennyson :

Crowned of music more than any son,
Voice of silver, song of gold,
Spirit soul and sense in unison :

Thine no lightning, thunder rolled,
But heav'n's light, the blue, the benison,
Grandeur of the gentle mould,
    Tennyson.

A SONG FOR BREAKFAST.

LADY MAUD, from yonder lime
    Thrice the hungry rook hath cawed,
Thrice hath heard the mantel chime,
    Lady Maud,

*Late for breakfast, lazy head,
Drowsy eight and dreamy nine,
Late to wake is late to bed.*

Morn hath been an hour abroad
Since I framed this simple rhyme;
Do you find the moral flawed?

*Latest rose is soonest shed,
Sickly grape and sorry wine,
Last to sleep is last to wed.*

Ah, you well may look sublime,
If a trifle overawed:
Better take the hint in time,
    Lady Maud.

A SONG IN DUDGEON.

I ORDERED tea: where is it? How the room is crammed,
And what a lot of women. "Cocoa?" Not for me,
I ordered—Waiter! There, he's off! the door is slammed—
  I ordered tea!

"Coming!" I know you're coming, *you* are! Let me see:
I've chopped and sandwiched, hammed and sandwiched, veal-and-hammed,
And not a drop to—Waiter!! "Coming!" So is *he*,

That other skulking idiot, stuffed with napkins, shammed
With starch and shirtfront from the necktie to the knee—
Waiter!!! "Oh 'ere you are, sir—coffee." Oh be d——d!
  I ORDERED TEA!

A SONG OF SCORN.

WHENCE all this mean contention?
    Whence
These vile disputes that make one sick,
Distinctions without difference
    'Twixt bric-a-brac and brac-a-bric?
    These plagues of gnats that sting and
        prick,
These wordy wars that make earth hell
    'Twixt fanatic and fanatic,
Betwixt brocade and brocatel?

Thence all your persecutions. Thence
    Your orthodox and heretic,
Your Prophet's beard and Peter's pence.
    Your presbytery and bishopric:
Dissensions between louse and tick,
    'Twixt infidel and infidel,
    'Twixt Protestant and Catholic,
Betwixt brocade and brocatel.

Hence, all electioneering! Hence
  Your squabbles, civic, politic!
A plague of both your Houses! Sense
  Might tell you thick head rancours thick.
When filthy grease burns with foul wick
What matters between stink and smell,
  Between Whig trick and Tory trick,
Betwixt brocade and brocatel?

Poet, whose fancies come too quick
  To mete to millionths of an ell,
Dispense thy verdict with a kick
  Betwixt brocade and brocatel.

A SONG FOR MY DARLING.

A BALLAD for my Sweet,
    Light as a dream forsaken,
A Ballad for her feet,
    Lest timely she should waken.
    Morn, by mist overtaken,
Seascape and landscape marling,
    From out his wings hath shaken
A Ballad for my Darling.

A Ballad of a day,
    And not a kiss within it,
Such as a maid may play
    And sing upon the spinet.
    And blackbird thrush and linnet
And swallow lark and starling
    Are waiting to begin it,
A Ballad for my Darling.

When fancy sighs in vain,
   Song well may slip his tether,
But let love hold the rein,
   He never turns a feather.
   What matter wind and weather,
Wild rain and tempest snarling?
   We sing, and all together,
A Ballad for my Darling.

Sweetheart, when daylight slips
   From cliff and scar and scarling,
He leaves upon sweet lips
   A Ballad for my Darling.

A SONG OF DAYDREAM.

GO, Ballad, fast as fancy flies,
    Outspeed my dreams across the brine,
And find my Lady where she lies,
    Else be no ballad more of mine.
    Tell her, in words like her divine,
The praises of her last for aye,
    Even if she live but in thy line,
O Ballad of a dreamy day.

O Ballad, Ballad, daylight dies,
    And dreams, like men, come home to dine;
And still my fasting fancy cries,
    And still I hunger for a sign.
    Where dost thou loiter, song supine,
What crest or headland bids thee stay,
    What Pyrenee or Apennine,
O Ballad of a dreamy day?

O Ballad, Ballad, from the skies
  A dawn at sunset thou dost shine ;
I read her music in those eyes,
  I know whose kiss hath perfumed thine.
Those lips, they are not red with wine,
Nor warm with sun, nor wet with spray,
  But with her lips of eglantine,
O Ballad of a dreamy day.

Sweet Heart, whose dreams are as a shrine
  Where others cross themselves and pray,
Take, take my meaning, and divine
  My Ballad of a dreamy day.

A SONG OF THE DANCE.

HUSH, hark! Beneath a moon as still
    As ever smiled on Paduan street
What rapture through the open sill
    Where music and the moonlight greet.
    O listen to the flying feet!
They pause, they falter, they refrain.
    Often as dance and music meet
Who but must wish them come again?

Once more, once more, the music shrill!
    Each soldier rising to the beat,
Each maiden answering with a will:
    They charge, they rally, they retreat.
    What matters dust or matters heat,
When blood and beauty fire the strain?
    When Mars and Venus are discreet,
Who but must wish them come again?

Wine, wine, wine, wine! Come, fill, fill, fill!
  Each warrior springing from his seat.
When smiles and kisses pay the bill,
  Who but may stand a comrade treat?
Who dreams of sleep or stays to eat
When love and wine are in the vein?
  When youth and pleasure are so sweet,
Who but must wish them come again?

Friend, in a world of oil and wheat
  The vines and bines may well remain:
When vetch and poppy are so sweet,
  Who but must wish them come again?

A SONG OF THE VINEYARD.

COME, Sweet, the morning clasps and
    closes
Her silver belt with sun sedate,
And kiss me where your vineyard dozes,
    A bowshot from the Saracen's Gate.
    One alley leadeth, straight as fate,
To greenest shade from golden shine :
    Come down in love as swift as hate,
And kiss me between leaves of vine.

Come, Sweet, it is the noon of roses,
    Thy lip is pregnant with their freight,
Each tendril by its leaf reposes,
    Vicenza and Verona wait.
    Though Paduan schools be learned and
        great,
Teach me a rarer lore of thine,
    Thy sizar here and graduate,
And kiss me between leaves of vine.

When midday sun as midnight snows is,
   May vines and roses bloom too late ;
When the vine-leaf as red as rose is,
   Are wine and kisses out of date.
   Bring to these lips of pomegranate
Thine own perfumed and red with wine,
   Cling as the grape-bunch to her mate,
And kiss me between leaves of vine.

Sweet, behind smiling leaves a-grate
   Veil all thy laughing eyes from mine,
But find beneath a parting strait,
   And kiss me between leaves of vine.

A SONG OF YES AND NO.

WHO says Come when my Love says Go?
   Who is free that she holds in jess?
Who laughs loud when she laughs low?
   Who keeps secret what she would guess?
   Who sows chickweed where she sows cress?
Who but must steer as she doth row?
   Who dare checkmate when she plays chess?
Who says Yes when my Love says No?

Who gives kiss when she answers blow:
   Who is bold that she would repress?
Who is a-cold when she doth glow:
   Who is coy that she would caress?
   Who binds up when she loosens tress:
Who but must ted as she doth mow?
   Who unrobes her when she would dress:
Who says Yes when my Love says No?

Who is dry if her springs do flow :
   Who is poor when she gives largess?
Who but must freeze when she doth. snow :
   Who but weep that she doth distress?
   Who hath sinned that she doth confess?
Who shall find friend that she finds foe?
   Who is cursèd that she shall bless?
Who says Yes when my Love says No?

Friend, be it guerdon, gift, or cess,
   Ill-come or welcome, weal or woe,
Who says No when my Love says Yes,
   Who says Yes when my Love says No?

www.ingramcontent.com/pod-product-compliance
Lightning Source LLC
Chambersburg PA
CBHW020847160426
43192CB00007B/816